ENTERTAINMENT GROUP

"MY DEEPEST PLEASURE"
BY
JAVON "CHIEF NETWORK" BATES

Published by: Dreamer Publishing/Tomahawk Entertainment Group
Written by: Javon Bates
Illustrated: Javon Bates
www.tomahawkentertainmentgroup.com

Javon "Chief Network" Bates is a self-made visionary who hails out of Cleveland, Ohio. Like any diamond in the rough, he has many facets to him that embody the ultimate entrepreneur. Javon has carved out a niche in the music industry, publishing industry, as well as the fragrance industry. As a writer, he has created personal memoirs of struggles in the urban community and collaborated with fellow writers such as Bruce Ballard to further the message. His works of poetry give you the true raw perspective of living through struggles as told in the collection of "THE JOURNEY" but also gives inspiring resolution to these issues as depicted in "HEAVEN CALLS" and "DO YOU WONDER WHY?" He doesn't only stop at poetry to reach his audience, by finding other artists much like him lyrically gifted and driven to succeed it only made sense for him to create his own entertainment group of radio, T.V., music, publishing, comedy, movies, and fashion. Marrying lyrics to original creative beats his music can only be described as musical bliss and sheer perfection! One might say this multi-faceted mogul shares his passion through whatever he does and above all his success comes from his relentless motivation to succeed and see others succeed with him on his journey through life.

<u>About the book</u>

My Deepest Pleasure reflects the true stories and thoughts of Javon Bates, his deep affection and personal attachment to his goal of reaching the hearts & minds of the reader. When you read a poem from his collection, you will anticipate 100% pure pleasure of your soul being touch with every word. He also gives advice to those who need it. He also mentions his tough and hard times but at the end, found something deeper than love it's MY DEEPEST PLEASURE!

My Dedication

I thank God first and foremost because I couldn't create this book without his help. I dedicate this book to My Deepest Pleasure "Monique Williams". I thank my mom, Javonna Bates, Dominque & Nak'ia Williams, my brothers of T.E.G. Bruce Ballard and Anthony Phillips Jr. I can't thank everyone personally by name but thanks to all my family, friends, fans, and followers of social media who believe in my vision and mission. If you are reading this, you made the dream a reality. THANKS!

MY DEEPEST PLEASURE

- What's Past Love? M.D.P.
  - 1st Sight
  - Tonight
- For A Woman…
  - 12 Roses
  - 15 Seconds
  - A Framed Angel
- A Perfect Summer Day
  - A Quote By Love
- A Time Of Depression
- A Valentines Message
- A Walk In My Shoes
- Afraid To Fail Or Succeed
  - Ambushed
  - Anniversary
- Another Bad Creation
- As Good As Money
  - Broken Pieces
  - Reparations
  - The Movement
  - No Just Us
  - The Stand
  - City Issues
  - New Father's
- The P.R.O.J.E.C.T.S.
  - Black His Story
  - Cause & Effect
- Dead, Broke and Starving
  - Don't Lose This

WHAT'S PAST LOVE? MY DEEPEST PLEASURE

What's beyond appreciation?

What's past infatuation?

What's above God's creation?

What's deeper than your heart? This requires your full
concentration

Where can I go past your mind for this information?

It's bigger than any life's donation

It's a feeling that has its own address and new location

That requires a lot of visual illustration

That new making love that requires a deep narration

Of seduction, touching, biting and tasting

Grabbing sheets, pillows and bodies oh….what a sensation

You will never witness this on video or any TV Station

This is a deep affection that, has a strong penetration

You will see my words on my body in quotation

Don't hold them too tight it might cut off the circulation

Our hearts talking to one another in this new translation

We line our bodies up together into a new formation

To feed our hunger of love and to leave starvation

We are aligned like stars in a constellation

What's over love in this civilization?

No lying, no cheating and no deceiving is the negotiation

If you break the rules of this pleasure, you will get a citation

What's deeper than love?

My deepest pleasure is the revelation!

^{1st} Sight

Was it love at first sight?

Or is it lust shining on us too bright

I think it is love because this feels too right

Which I've seen my feelings grow to new heights

This love is like drinking from the fountain of youth

You got my heart beating heavily and no doubt, that's the truth

When I see your face

It makes me feel like I'm right in place

When I don't see you it feels like I'm in a race

I want to stick to you girl like tape or paste

No matter the weight, size, or race

I'm still going to continue to chase

You down for that love that can't be erased

Or misplaced

But I love to see that look on your face

When you opened your heart up and I got a taste

Of your personality and your style

You meet the standards of a goddess profile

I can be the best man you ever had because I really know how

This love hitting me like bullets, *pop, pop, pop*...POW!

I'm bleeding joy and happiness

This is real love no need to imagine this

<u>Tonight</u>

Can you come over tonight?

I don't know yet let me make sure everything is going to be all right

I made your favorite dish

And tonight I'm going to grant every fantasy and wish

It sounds tempting

But did I forget to mention

I got to go to college in the morning

And I can't go there yawning

I promise it won't be boring

It's my love that I'll be pouring

And energy I'll be storing

It's your body I'll be touring

Letting my mouth do all the exploring

It's satisfaction I'm ensuring

Tonight it's you I'll be escorting

To ecstasy and I'm a MVP like Michael Jordan

When it comes to making love that's so important

It's the full version never shorten

And go on and on and on and on

Till it's nothing left on the bone

It was a long flight I done flown

Through at least 3 or 4 time zones

It can only be one of a kind

It's eternity and you are always on my mind

4 A Woman...

This is for the mother

And the sister who can also be a brother

If needed to be a king

But her title is better known as a queen

She is confident with her jeans filled with high self-esteem

Only she can birth a dream

Another living and walking human being

If you look at her you will see why men always fiend

For her beauty and finesse is what you've witnessed and you've seen...

12 Roses

This is my bouquet

Full of roses and love to let you know that everything will be okay

That's the reason why we celebrate your life beyond today

It really means so much more than words can really say

This is your hour and you have brightened our day

We will always miss you and we've enjoyed your stay

We miss your beautiful smile

Your technique and that model profile

You leave us here with hope and trust which was always your style

It might be the end of the race but never your final mile...

15 Seconds

For 15 seconds I saw your face

You made my eyes go on a chase

It don't matter about your religion or race

The feeling was like shoe strings as you begin to lace

My heart with warmth and grace

Your complexion was the type I would love to taste

But if I let you go past these feelings will be a waste

I can only keep these thoughts up by using love for paste

And cutting out pictures of you and hang them all over the place

When you smiled that 15 seconds sprayed on me like a can of mace

It was like you were red roses in my vase

Or like the best business plan in my briefcase

Or like a R&B song with enough treble and bass

Your beauty is like a painting I wish I could sit down and trace

You amazed me

In just that little bit of time it's driving me crazy

It's leaving me hot like a flame

And I'm still wondering what's your name?

A Framed Angel

This is for protection from all evil

An angel sent to protect God's people

Hanging around in any situation

To deliver us from demons sent by Satan

An angel sent to watch our homes and holy places

He's securing all ages and races

This is an angel in a frame

To work for and glorify his wonderful name

A Perfect Summer Day

A good day starts with sunshine and clear blue skies

Nobody fighting, getting hurt, and nobody dies

Nothing but happiness and no one cries

Just a peaceful morning, man what a surprise

Flowers blooming and children growing as time flies

Watch the season change as summer says its bye-byes

A Quote By Love

You got to love yourself

Before you can love somebody else

True love starts within

Let confidence, hope, ambition, and self-esteem begin

To overcome depression with a win

Hold your head high and never let down your chin

That's how we survive day by day as women and men

A Time Of Depression

I know you're on your last leg

On you're last strings

On your last hopes

On your last dream

But it's time to redeem

All the good things that life will bring

Valentine's Message

It's your heart and beauty I continue to chase

To capture it and bring it to this special place

Of love on this special day

Thinking will we still be together, I hope and pray

It's a whole lot I can really say

About how much I care and I love you in this special way

It's you I always think about day by day

Loving you is the price I'll be willing to pay

This is all my love sitting on this tray

Prepared and written on paper for you on Valentine's Day

A Walk In My Shoes

My shoes say they're size 12s

I've been in and out hell

But I never been to jail

Only lock up in this cell

Called life and it's a crazy tale

Look at all the times I done failed

Will his poetry sell?

Or will they boot him like a Dell?

Computer system as well

They worry about 5 kids I feed

Is he selling cocaine or weed?

My kids never have a want or need

Because they know every day, I bleed

So I just increase my speed

To keep up and maintain my lead

In this thing I see

Many cigarette packages I see

People losing their wife and their families

To work, liquor, and exotic fantasies

Can anybody in this galaxy

Fit my shoes like me

People hate when I write about my honesty

I did live in poverty

And spent all my money on this lottery

Called Poetry it's an art like pottery

Please take off my shoes give me back my property!

To Fail or Succeed

It will never change like the seasons

Or change like the weather

Or change like a tire

It only gets better

Day by day

Week by week

Month to month

Until it gets to its peak

Running until it can't go no further

So many reasons it dies

But is it a murder?

Everything is on the line

Your hopes and wishes

Just ambition is available at this present time

Starving for many years

Empty bowls and dishes

And tears of fear

This is what I really need

To accept

But am I afraid to fail or to succeed?

Ambushed

"Oh yes"

They tried to leave me in a bloody mess

Cutting my throat but first they shot me in the chest

"We were all supposed to be from the same flesh"

But they jumped me like a game of checkers with the strategy of chess

They were paparazzi's who started their own news press

They're spreading news about me I guess

But it's you they want to impress

Adding extra people to the situation but I boycott and protest

Anything they do physically and mentally unless

They keep that trap shut so we can finally progress

The things at hand that I need to address

The issues and negative vibes that I need to suppress

The more they hate the more I get blessed

You're all dead wrong that's what I must confess

Your goal is to try to end my career and my happiness

But God made me a blueprint for my achievements and success

To conquer this journey and your horrible conquest

You need to go and find you a life in the Valley that's what I suggest

Your not even on my level you're something much, much less

Now everybody knows from the North, South, East, and West

That I passed your class and I aced your test

And I took first place in this poetic contest

<u>Anniversary</u>

This is a celebration between a man and a woman in love with each other

If love was a crayon, that would be our sacred color

If it were a song, our picture would be on that CD cover

If it were candy, we would be that favorite charm sucker

If it were a movie, it would be on every shelf at blockbuster

Are we the product or the customer?

It doesn't matter because love is our supplier and our hustler

Selling us high hopes and romantic passion

Leaving us with a day of achievements and 100% satisfaction

With plenty additions and no subtractions

All you hear is love screaming and clapping

A day with no hate and no egos clashing

We're always wearing love's latest fashion

The word Anniversary and please keep that in action

Happy Anniversary!

Another Bad Creation

He woke up with a surprise

Hot grits upon his eyes

Sticking to his skin crying but he realized

All the hate, anger, pain, and lies

Putting bruises upon her face, chest, and thighs

Leaving mental scars for the rest of our lives

Chewing through her heart like hot apple pies

Her heart crashing like that car from "Vanilla Skies"

All the rage and torment buzzing through her brain like bees and flies

He never sat down and analyze

The "American Beauty" who has no "Family Ties"

This time no "Family Matters"

To your "60 Seconds" of beatings with your own Dan Rather

Or not you're ready for verbal or physical confrontation

Having to face her humiliation

She was sick of being a victim of frustration

She wished she were the "Six degrees of Separation"

From him, but this is no demonstration

That's right; love and hate have no relation

No specific time or affiliation

He has been placed in love's probation

And she's lock up for assault and 20 years is what she's facing

She left her man looking like Freddy Krueger or Jason

So he better find Johnny Cochran or somebody close to Perry Mason

It's forever in her head and there will be no erasing

She's another victim a monster in the making...

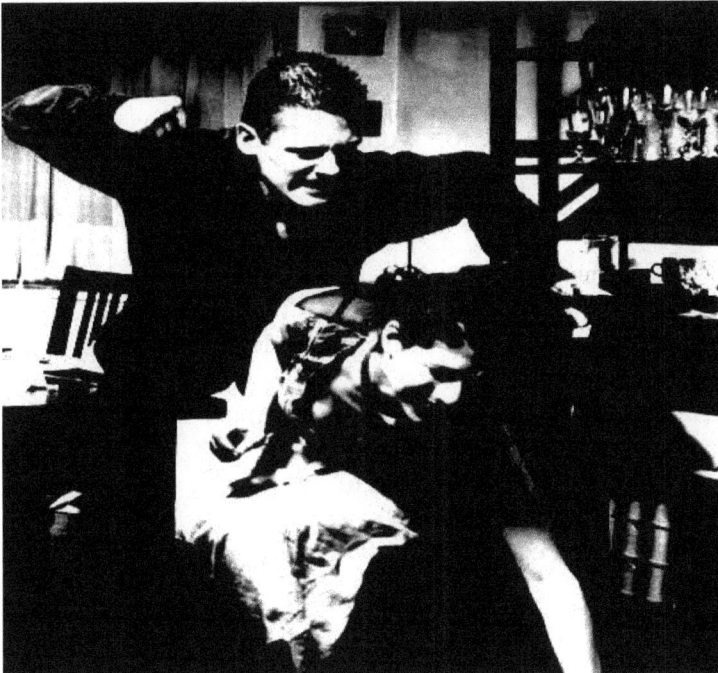

As Good As Money

This is my recognition

To express how I feel about your great character and position

Thank you for taking the time out to listen

To the story of an extraordinary journey and expedition

Of a woman who is loves first edition

She's love's statement and only mission

She's that home cooked meal out the kitchen

She's the top woman of her division

She cut straight to the heart like an incision

She has a diamond soul with a motherly vision

She's not perfect but I know I made the right decision

I thank her for giving

Me a chance to start living

In her heart and I'm not forgetting

About her qualities and traits that are in her heart patently sitting

Storing my honesty, trust, and love is what I'm submitting

In this envelope that you can put on like a mitten

It's not game, it's the truth is what I'm SPITTING!

Broken Pieces

I know it's been rough for the both of us

But I'm sorry and all I want is your honesty and trust

It was anger speaking and talking

I'm tired of that he say she say barking

We are supposed to be like sister and brother

But when you said those two words you expect to get treated like no other

I apologized for getting in your face

This whole event was like a total disgrace

I admit that I got out of hand

But believe me I would never lay a hand

On you and I do care

But I think you made this situation unfair

Please come with reason and fact

Not with I heard and they say all of that

We could have spoken one on one

And remember hate loves no one

I never called you out you name

Disrespect you or try to destroy your name

I'm sorry if I hurt your heart

I want to try to build back what was torn apart

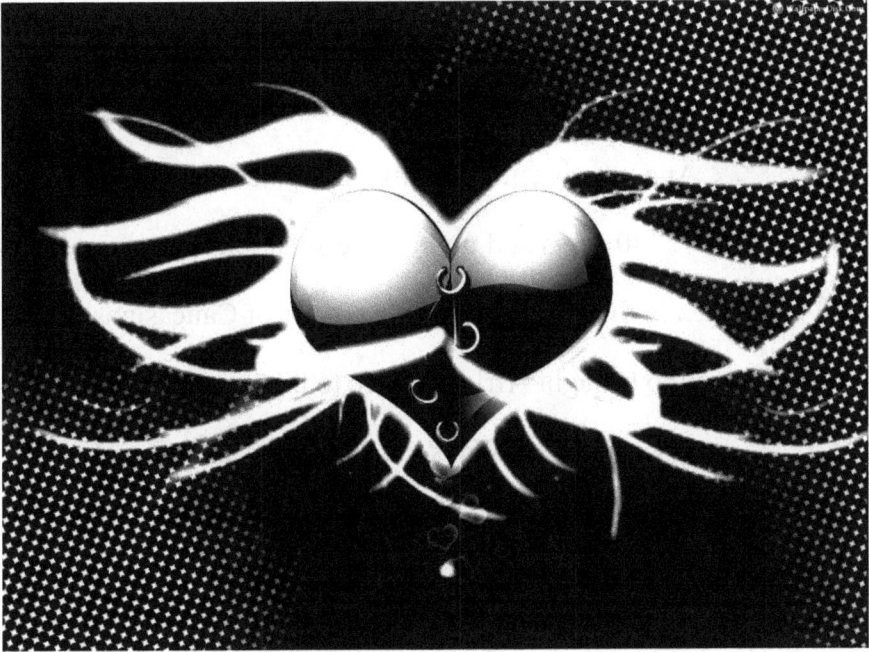

Reparations

This is my translation

Of my forefathers who were slaves in this federation

Which were hung for starting schools and church congregations

And who is entitled for their reparations?

40 acres and mule is the situation

Written in the constitution by a couple of Caucasians

Who brought African's here to this nation?

It wasn't Australians, duchess, or Asians

It wasn't Puerto Ricans, Cubans, or Jamaicans

It was Africa's first invasion

That led to this struggle of us working on plantations

Raping our great mothers causing fornication

And they wonder why we made the Rainbow Coalition,
NAACP, and Black Farmer organizations

That later on constructed other African-American Affiliations

That later on gave us our own T.V. stations

We had to go through a few whips, lynching, hangings, and many
body lacerations

Guess who made you money for your cotton operations?

Now we got Obama, Oprah, Jay-Z, you, and me to inflate our
urban population

With money, power, respect, and many dedications

The Movement

What happen to all the meetings and all the marches?

What happen to the future Martin Luther King's, Malcolm X's and Rosa Park's?

Now it's Pimps and prostitutes serving billions like the golden arches

What happen to break dancing, spray paint, and black magic markers?

I'm talking about before Chrysler Newport's, Ninety-Eights and Dodge Chargers

I'm talking about keeping pictures of Marvin Gaye and Diana Ross in our lockers

Going to New York to see the famous Harlem Globetrotters

The days of wearing Chuck Taylor's and Dr. J's and not yet the S dot Carter's

Joining the NAACP or the Black Panthers when times were getting harder

As they sprayed us with water hoses because the black voice was getting louder

The quote of "We shall overcome" became our power

As we listened to The Temptations, The Stylistics, and Al Green on the radio every hour

Fredrick Douglas, Booker T. Washington, and Marcus Garvey
was like our Bill Cower

Coaching a team of activists which are now black entrepreneurs
and architects who can build towers

Because of a dream now, our talents and achievements finally
begin to shower

No Just Us

They say justice is blind

So I put on eyeglasses to find

The truth, which is behind

Every single word and every little line

That was taken from my grandmother's mind

When she marched in D.C. with a sign

It was the African-American design

For equal rights for all man kind

Go home "nigger" was there favorite line

Used, when they had the time

To leave their jobs early for this important climb

In history, the police reported this act as a crime

Like our boycotts and protesting, we had to pay a fine

The fine was death to a few family members of mine

God bless

But they will never properly rest

In peace, only by a piece

That's why they are considered deceased

The Stand
Javon Bates..Walking to the podium.....
"Lady's and gentlemen"

This is for those people who said poetry would never be

But don't forget poetry lives through me

Because it's me and we are thee

Most mistreated and hated

Form of writing but now you see we are underrated

We help feed the uneducated

This is like orange juice but it's not concentrated

I was here you just never appreciated

The spoken word or rap song that I previously created

Even if I sold one book, I still made it

Inside of a mind that is not saturated

But infatuated

By my expressions that are verbally fabricated

Like a suit jacket

That is loud that makes a lot of racket

I set up a brand new bracket

And I created a demand that was so rapid

Using my skills as my only gadget

33

I'm the new father of this bastard

They call me poetry

With no publicity

No buzz around your city

So I got sick of this pity

And got dirty and gritty

They want to ask me questions like I'm fifty

Pitches away from striking out a Ken Griffey

I'm homemade you can't call me Jiffy

Cornbread, because who's future is looking iffy

I'm making a stand right here and it aren't going to be pretty

Who is with me or against me?

New Father's

It's the most underrated day of the year

Being a father is like having a career

People think we all about partying, smoking, and drinking beer

So this particular case I'm going to make myself clear

About true fathers no need to look we right here!

The fathers of the new generation

The kind that take care of their families with no hesitation

The fathers with poise and dedication

A father who is great with family participation

He's not just child support he's a father in this situation

He's a leader for a son or daughter and the whole human population

A role model for any child or family organization

He's not just making kids and supplying the nation

With fatherless children living in starvation

He's supporting his kids or loved ones through all the frustration

He's not perfect but he maintains a good reputation

Through his love, respect, talents, and communication

The P.R.O.J.E.C.T.S.

(People **R**elaying **O**n **J**ust **E**nough **C**ash **T**o **S**urvive**)**

Meanwhile... in Black America...

We living in a world full of madness

Full of hate, terror, and sadness

We living in poverty sleeping on an old mattress

Full of holes but I'm trying to maintain some gladness

I'm stuck in a society full of badness

Full of drugs, ignorance, and flashiness

People who ignore children begging for a little happiness

They just want help to get them a little success

To try to be the best in life nothing less

Every day we write letters but still no answer from the congress

It feels like we aren't making any progress

So these are the things we suggest

It feels like the government taking all the eggs from our nest

Putting all the killers, drug dealers, and prostitutes in the projects

Giving them curfews, too many rules, and no privacy so what's next?

The ghetto ain't nothing to them but a bunch of business checks

Many urban disrespects

Unemployed, bootlegging, and trafficking connects

We are individuals with good intellects

This is our life with no makeup and no special effects

Full of robberies, violence, predators, and unprotected sex

Even the innocent people here are suspects

Of driving in nice cars and the police planting objects

Because they were millionaires working hard and living complex

They consider us as being an urban subject

Who was never made to direct

Or to make our own decisions that we select

It's three things they fear from us is money, power, and respect

Too much of those things might cause ropes around our necks

But I'm just trying to stand tall like a Tyrannosaurus Rex

To grow the seeds of our leaders like Harriet, Fredrick, Martin, Huey, and Malcolm X

It's time to put an end to this generation hex

Black: His Story

This is our history

All we get is a month for our struggles and misery?

Who really killed Tupac and Biggie, it remains a mystery

Was it really Thomas Edison who created electricity?

Why we can't get on the dollar bill to get some publicity

Why we can't walk in groups without the store calling security?

Why they want to test our character and maturity?

Why we can't get a monument or a statue of liberty?

Because we live in the projects or the ghetto, we have no
innocence or purity?

We're famous for sports and entertainment, and not going to an old
prison facility

We're receiving Grammy's, Emmy's, and music awards for our
creditability

This month represents our only time in America to respect and
honor our creativity

To end and ceased the drama and negativity

To expand more black history positively

Not just in the hood also in the suburbs and the inner city

We learn something dark can be wonderful and filled with beauty

We're the color of Ebony with the Essence that's so truly

Dead, Broke, and Starving

I starve to eat later

I can't depend on this elephant because he's a traitor

He's adding souls to devils calculator

Who's the one with the bad behavior?

I can only depend on Jesus Christ my lord and savior

I can't count on the government to put me in labor

Calling themselves doing me a favor

They don't want me to buy a new Lincoln Navigator

They don't want me to buy a home; they want me in a trailer

They want me on the block to destroy my neighbor

They want me to be the same and not an innovator

They're making us live like we're terminators

But we're not in a movie with Arnold Schwarzenegger

They don't want us to be millionaires they want us to be a borrowers and a beggars

Have us being harassed by creditors and bill collectors

We want to be real stators and investors

We want to be doctors, teachers, and professors

Just give us our dreams nothing lesser

They want us dead and broke they want us starving

Don't Lose This...

I'm feeling your mind

I'm feeling your soul

I'm feeling your heart

But I got to know

Is it the same?

Am I to blame?

The way my love came

Upon you like a hurricane

Through the wind and the rain

The way love grabbed you I can't explain

The way we linked, we are like a chain

We're photographic like a picture in a frame

I'm the red stripe and you're the candy cane

You're the wick and I'm the flame

Exploding love across our names

Flying to newer levels of love like an airplane

Having my heart pacing fast like a train

At last it's you and love I must keep in my heart and maintain

<u>Everlasting</u>

Love is not just a word it's an action

It's a hug, a kiss, a poem, a card, and an affectionate reaction

Not to be confused as a distraction

It's my heart for yours in this love transaction

I know it feels like I'm slipping but I use your heart for my traction

I don't know why my heart is collapsing

Does he love me is what your probably asking?

I do because our love is outlasting

It's still full of joy, happiness, and passion

Its just stress giving me a crazy reaction

But you're the answer to this love fraction

Divided by us and there will be no need for subtraction

I promise you love and a 100% satisfaction

Whatever the amount of love you put down, I'm matching

We don't need no scripts, no scenes, and no director it's reality for us no acting

I want to spend my life with a love that is everlasting

Extraordinary

You're so extraordinary

I couldn't define you even with a dictionary

But this love is never scary

You're sweet like chocolate strawberries

The body spray you wear smell exactly like wild cherries

You got me checking you out like a book at the library

You got the status beyond Beyoncé and Halle Berry

You bring me love and joy like Mary

J. Blige with a twist of love that is very

Unique and irresistible

I'm so addicted to your love that it's critical

When I'm lonely, I feel kind of pitiful

But when I see you again I stop feeling miserable

I thank you God for sending me a living miracle

Someone I can love and adore in the physical

It's not just about feelings; I love you in general

You're my vitamin, my heavenly mineral

Failure Is Not An Option-

Failure is not an option

Look into my eyes and success is what you will be watching

All the pain, sleepless nights, and struggles will never be forgotten

I remember that day I told success "please don't stop knocking"

I opened my door and all these wonderful achievements just started dropping

Because of my dedication and motivation there will be no stopping

My words and my voice

I choose freedom, poetry, and confidence as my choice

To live and die by daily

I treat it like my wife, my mother, or my baby

If something happens to it, I might go crazy

It can only love me back and never hate me

I thank God what you have done for me lately

You brought me out of my mental and financial slavery

You made me a role model and never made me lazy

You created a possibility not a wish, not a could have, or a maybe

Father's Day

For the man who carried our family through its pain

Always finding a way to get us out the rain

Teaching us how to deal with heartbreaks and shame

Holding us together through his highlights and fame

Every year in June we celebrate your day and name

Remembering all the wonderful days and years in this special frame

Symbolizing what every family should want to gain

Day after day many glad you came

A man who can handle stress without going insane

Yes, I thank God for a real father that I can claim

<u>Genesis</u>

I can see beyond what I've been seeing

Sadness was just a way of being

I found out the true meaning

Of nothing, but that's why I'm freeing

The past from my way of speaking

It's something that was revealed in one weekend

I am the beholder except for when internally sleeping

Open your eyes and let yourself do the teaching

Manifesting and preaching

Do a lot more of loving and reaching

Out to others

Not just to your sisters and brothers

Cousins, uncles, aunts, fathers, and mothers

Grow relationships to form friends and something other...

Heads Or His Tales

What do you do when you see that it's coming?

Do you continue to hide or do you keep on running?

Do you sing the song or do you keep on humming?

It's hard to stop eating but I keep on munching

It feels like my heart is doing all the kicking and punching

Listen to me don't make no assumption

But it's hard when you keep my blood pumping

I want you to feel that you do mean something!

Sorry if I made you feel like you were nothing

The reason is because I don't really know who I'm loving

It's really #^$*ed up and it's got me bugging

When I'm with her it's you, I'm really hugging

And it's your heart that I'm really touching

I try to ignore it but it just keeps on dubbing

I keep on scratching it and rubbing

It's hot and ready to come out the oven

Should I listen to God or to the devil's instructions?

In my mind the situation was exploding like a volcano eruption

I was actually hoping for a delay or an interruption

But all I got was some bad vibes and some lustful corruption

Is this really love or is this just a good seduction

It's a bad predicament because you're reading about my friend's cousin

Who is now divorce because he broke the laws of a husband

These are his words, his thoughts, and his cussing

He wanted me to tell you that he's sorry for the fighting and fussing

And he knows that the things that he did was wrong and disgusting

Heavenly Tissue

It's so many things we can say

As we sit here and mourn today

Thinking about all the good things

Wishing today was just a bad dream

Please remain strong

And find a shoulder to lean on

With the heart of no failures and no fears

Just a soul with our heavenly father for the rest of our years

This is my tissue to wipe away all of your tears

He's celebrating with our late love ones and other peers

And we celebrating his life on earth with so many claps and cheers

I Am

Poetry

I live, I breathe, I see

I talk, I eat, I be,

The cause, the reason, the words of reality

Every stroke of the pen I'm that tragedy

I'm that who, that what, that cry

I'm that <u>P</u> that <u>O</u> that <u>E</u> that <u>M</u> that's why

I fill these books with a lot of U's and I's

I need those ears, those hearts, and those eyes

To follow my hopes, my struggles, my dreams, and
my tries

My hurts, my pain, my love, their lies

Me, a body of poetry that will never die

I Promise...

I don't want to ever lose your loving

Don't leave me without any kissing or no hugging

I did this all for you and not just for nothing

I did all this running around don't you hear me huffing and puffing

Today's topic is love and that's all we're discussing

Let's just take our time no need for rushing

Fist fighting or cussing

That's enough hate to leave this love in a concussion

Causing us hell and a lot of interruptions

All you going to hear is, a lot of talk and no hushing

A couple of rumors and some heart crushing

I came to cure your cold like I'm Robitussin

That cold chill of hate

Who is trying to leave you sick and your heart is losing major weight

Drink my love by the gallon it's healthy like V8

So please don't be late

If love told you to meet around 7 or 8

Please, please, don't be afraid

To receive my love like a check you about to get paid

In full trust, honesty, and loyalty

I promise to treat you the best because you represent nothing but royalty

I Witness Love

It was like a dream, it felt unbelievable

I witness a love that was receivable

It was full of life and unbeatable

Some say it's hard to explain and it's unspeakable

But love is spiritual food that we need as people

If hate was your first movie let love be your sequel

Let me be that line

That connects hearts and minds

Let me be that quote

That gave your heart love and hope

Let me be that sound

Behind the words that will pound and pound

Like a heart beating

Through the walls of pain and those hands are still bleeding

And they are still needing

A lot of healing and believing

I do understand the grieving

But we have to put that aside to start achieving

Which is the topic love once again

All of my love is possessed in every stroke of the pen

Every single thought explained within

Written and placed on my heart from beginning to end

And this is all the love that I want to send

To you my brother, my sister, my girlfriend, my family and all my friends

I...

I miss you

I really do

I miss the times I spent with you

You were the realest thing to me

You brought great smiles to see

You were like a brother to some degree

But so caring like a friend should always be

It's been nothing but good times

And to remember you with these good lines

I still got love in my heart, soul, and mind

I just want to tell you I still think about you all the time

I'm just sitting here letting the pen cry

The tears of my words running down my letter... I

I'm Leaving

No matter what you say to me

You can't change the way I see

You talk about how love can be

I want to be love more frequently

Not just for an hour not on Friday

If this act continues, you're going to learn the hard way

What happened to the love that was heading our way?

I took it for real while you laughed and played

I can't take any more of this heart breaking display

So I packed up and left you alone today

And forever I might say

All the love that you wasted and now you're going to pay

Is it over?

It breaks my soul

To see a crushed plan or an injured goal

Or a damaged dream

With no shoulder for you to lean

When you're sad or you need to blow some steam

Each tear represents a struggle or a problem

Looking to God just knowing he can solve them

It's all pain, stress, and shame

You feel like it's all your fought because you have no one else to blame

Thinking to yourself how last year left and came

It feels like your life's on pause and it's not a game

Still feel shackled up with this mental chain

Waiting for the sun to shine so it can end this hurtful rain

Look What Love Sent

You're a gift from love

Which means you're a work of the creator above

You were built to last

Through this hate, war, struggles, and whatever will past

You're like a luxury car with a full tank of gas

Inside your car, you can hear the rhythms of R&B, Poetry, and Jazz

Nice lengthy hair with beautiful skin the color of brass

You send my heart explosions the impact of a nuclear blast

You're the newest line of love's fashion

Which you caught my attention for this main attraction

Love has taught us how to live together, build together, and stick together

To lead us to a better future with his powers together forever...

Love Connection

Loving and caring

That's why I love starring

At your face because love's glaring

From your heart do you mind sharing

Some of that love because mine is tearing

Your love is one of a kind there's no comparing

To the kind you keep on spreading

Too your mind and soul is the direction that I'm heading

To land on your heart love's favorite section

While you got me on hold waiting for loves connection

Love Wonders?

You can't go pick this off a tree

Can't bake it or wrap it and place it under a tree

The word describes you and me

The four-letter word spelled l-o-v-e

Can you smell it?

Can you taste it?

Because if you have it

Don't waste it

The love between your son and daughter

Mother and father

Sister and brother

Husband and wife

The people who you should love for life

But we understand about love and its plans

About its actions and your demands

But you know that it's in command

On a large ground where it will expand

You can try to stop it

Or do whatever you can

But remember it can be an enemy or your best friend

Can't predict love like the weather man

It takes time for you to understand

The Who's. What's, and Why's

And the Kleenex full of cries

Mind, Body, And Soul

I want to rip off all your clothes

Starting from your shirt down to your toes

Touching those spots nobody knows

We can make love fast or slow

You can get on top and take control

You can slide up and down that pole

You know

I can go

All night until the Sun, glows

It's hot in here for shows

Like we making love on hot coals

But getting you in your birthday suit is my whole goal

I'm trying to get your hormones working on swoll

You already got my mind going out of control

The way my tongue travels on your body I had to pay a body toll

Holding your body like a hungry man hugged up on a cereal bowl

All you feel in this place is mind, body, and soul

Loves taste is so sweet and chewy like a Tootsie Roll

Miss Saturday

Her eyes were the most beautiful pair I ever seen

She has the most perfect curves and shape for those blue jeans

I know need to draft her for my fantasy team

She just don't shine man she BLING!

When she walks, I hear her shoes sing

Me a love song that perfect three part harmony

When she walks, it's like she's marching with an army

So I stop like a red light

A she walk's past but I lose focus and my eyesight

My first thought in my head was "I need to get right"

Because I'm on the wrong side and on the wrong flight

I need to get to that city

Where everything is fine, blessed, and pretty

Missing

I'm missing y'all

I will be there if you trip or fall

If you need me, you can always call

I'm your father, your dad you can have it all

Whatever you need I give it short or tall

I got my heart-felt words spray-painted on this wall

I love you all no matter if you big or small

This love is beyond child support and shopping at mall

It's me cooking meals with my girls and me and my son playing football

All I can do is think of the good times that God installed

But it's one thing that I will never do is stall

If you were in trouble or in a brawl

Remember I'm your father no matter what the situation and I hope you understand it all

Mission: Your Heart

I'm sorry for being so stupid lately

I always recognized you're a wonderful lady

It's your love that made me stop acting crazy

And I apologize for being lazy

It's just a few things on my mind making me shaky

I'm just hoping you forgive me and not hate me

For the things that I've did so daringly

I'm asking for forgiveness and not charity

I'm using love in this moment of clarity

It's amazing that I'm holding on to you barely

I mean it when I say that I will treat you more fairly

I love you and I'm signing this sincerely

Yours forever

Love's hidden treasure

Love's vision

Do you accept this heart felt mission?

My Brother

My brother

Is like no other

He shines today in a brand new color

The color that represents a friend and a son of a mother

Who has God now to comfort him with his heavenly cover

Today I'm going to spread his name over the world like butter

I know that your new life has just begun

But you left behind a Christmas present for me, which is your only
son

My Deepest Pleasure

The smooth surface of her body

Had me drunk like I was drinking a bottle of Bacardi

It was just her and me in this stripping party

I wanted to turn her body into my new hobby

It can go down near the lake, on the elevator, or the hotel lobby

Will she explode? Most likely, probably!

Her touch was so convincing and softly

Her body was mine she didn't act stingy or snobby

But I beat that up like I was performing martial arts, Kung Fu, or karate

The way I took her body in my hands, you can
consider that aggravated robbery

Or assault with a deadly weapon while riding on my Harley

The kind of loving that's like hot cheese melted on fresh broccoli

This is the making of an original sex video not a bootleg copy

You can be my mamacita and I can be your poppy

As I inject you with my personal piece of property

He's standing strong, tall, big, and cocky

They call him a black stallion in the ring like "Rocky"

A construction worker knocking down walls and laying pipe is his philosophy

He's a master of love making with the right massages and geography

With the right stroke of the pen, you will need psychology

Because I'm equip. with 6 pieces of love hi-technology

Sorry, I leave these words as my flowers and my deepest apology…

My Token

My heart

My tears

For you I hear

Your mind so clear

And my hands they cheer

This feeling is from year to year

You make me smile from ear to ear

You make me conquer all my fears

I use my poetry for tissue to wipe those tears

I need to increase my love as I change these gears

I traveled looking for love and then you appeared

I like this change; you're my new career

This is spoken with so much feeling and I'm so sincere

This my engagement, our world premiere

This love is so intense and it can be severe

To walk you through my heart and love is near

The journey of life, which is our love frontier

Don't be afraid let go of the wheel so I can steer

You to any question that was unclear

I got the answer in my heart tucked right here!

People Change Like The Weather

Sometimes I wake up to a thunder

But I saw sunshine with no clouds, it used to make me wonder

Will it stay calm or will a flood take me under?

It's snowing today and yesterday just felt like summer

I couldn't predict the weather so I felt dumber and dumber

Until one day, I got the weather line number

Which gave me predictions for fall, winter, spring, and summer

Summer was when she was in a good mood

Fall was when she wanted to get smart with me and be rude

Spring was us going out to the movies and her preparing home cooked food

Winter was her not clapping or cheering for me, I was just getting booed

She put a cloud of darkness upon me for the last time

But when I left her, she felt the heat as the Lord let the sun shine...

Poetic Animation

A woman wants to be loved, touched, and respected

Not hated, abused, and neglected

She's so honorable and never will be disrespected

She solves my problems when things are getting hectic

She's my nurse, my doctor, and my medic

She's my aspirin for my headache

She's my sun and my moon

She makes it feel warm like the month of June

She's the main attraction for this afternoon

She's like flowers I love to watch her heart bloom

I love to see her face full of love and not gloom

And I hope to reunite with her real soon

To express the feelings of this poetic cartoon

Called love and nothing will attack our love platoon

Except for the minds of two hearts going boom!

The impact swept me off my feet like a broom

Reason For My Insanity

They tried to burn my name

Have my name to never be the same

Said my name to be the blame

It's not funny it's my life it's not a game

Say what you want, bring the pain!

I changed my mind state to insane

Chaos from here to Maine

A few scratches, cuts, and bloodstains

Through all the B.S., headaches, and migraines

I fight my terrorist on airplanes

Tied up on a track while you driving the train

With words running through my veins

They saying my name in vain

Through this is how I explain

The glory, love, hate, and change

<u>Recovering From A Tragic Death</u>

I feel your pain from in my heart

I know it's like a piece of puzzle taken apart

From you and your family tree

But now a soul is living heavenly

And happily ever after

With God, full of joy and laughter

We can now gather

All the moments and pictures that matter

On earth, it was a soul that was lost

But at least a soul won with God the boss

Rumors

I'm glad you're reading this statement

I want to make sure your face hit the pavement

From these words of amazement

Stories of me sleeping with who and where I pay rent

Fighting to spread rumors on me creating an augment

Go get a life, you evicted, you not my resident

Matter of fact go and grieve this to your union president

Tell them how much time you spent

Following me like Twitter, don't be hesitant

Go take some pictures and post them like it's evidence

But do I care what you do is that relevant?

Y'all Stab me in my back

I heard that pistol go click… clack

You took my name and never put it back

Set it on fire and hung my heart up like it was a plaque

What I do to deserve a hit of that?

As I lay on the ground lifeless and flat

Y'all want to find news like a crack head looking for crack

But this is my answer my verbal smack!

If this was a song "Ether" would be the name of this track

I can take all your trash, bullets, talk and all that

And I'm going to leave you with this last line

I was the one who saw you and you were blind the whole time!

The Answer Or The Question?

Baby, why we keep breaking up like cheap cell phone reception?

Why argue and fight, that's not the right selection

For couples to choose, I thought we learned our lesson

When we both were locked up that was so depressing

Locked up in hate not jail that's why I'm expressing

That I truly realize that you are actually my blessing

So we can stop all the drama and games, that's all I'm requesting

If not, next time I will hit you with love as my weapon

Hopefully to gather us together one day at a wedding

To never have your heart play the blues like Otis Redding

I'm thinking of love as the direction we should be heading

But is love the answer or is it the question?

The Approach

Who's that lady?

Will I get to know her? Maybe

So I decide to walk in her direction

I will take no let downs or no deceptions

So I came closer to her so I can see her eyes

Her beauty never subtracted it just multiplies

I told her forgive me for starring I apologize

For your elegance, you made me realize

The features of a wonderful creature from the heavenly skies

And God was right beauty never dies

I found out where it lies

Inside a person beyond the makeup and nice thighs

Those Lips left me in space like I was on the Enterprise

Spaceship once again her smile left me all surprised

All I know that infatuation was on the rise

So If I earn your heart being in love with you will be my prize

But right now it's a dream all I can do is fantasize

So I will just pull out love's plan, study, recite, and strategize

The Breakup...

Where's the love at?

I see we got a lot of blood on the front door mat

Communication is the situation where you and me stand at

Our relationship is like drug rehab, it's on crack

Enough fussing, cussing, and cheating and all that

We don't eat together

Sleep together

Only thing we do is cheat and hit the street together

This is a war fought in snow and stormy weather

This was suppose to be for worse or for better

The good book said we supposed to be together forever

But now I guess it's whatever

You caught me cheating with your friends and you're right I wasn't
too clever

I'm sorry about the lipstick and perfume smells off my sweater

I want to go back to when I first met cha'

Take you to the movies and that place where I first fed ya'

From platinum necklaces to diamond rings

From Red lobster to Burger King

Everything isn't always what it seems

At one point, I was your king

Sitting on the throne and you was that queen

I'm taking my pride and packing all my things

My visions, my sins, my fantasies, and all my dreams

The Ceremony

We join today to celebrate a wedding

Together forever is the direction they will be heading

There will be a lot of butterflies and sweating

But don't worry love is their secret weapon

We got 2 diamond rings

For today's king and queen

On their throne surrounded by love and this is not a dream

This is not a fake or a copy it's the real thing

This love is forever and not a one-day fling

They will enjoy the gifts of life that God will bring

To bloom like a flower growing in spring

Always and forever is what their hearts will SING!

The Conversation

I'm back with the right approach

And this time I got love as my coach

Love found me when I was lost

But I found you and your heart was the cost

I paid for waiting patiently

Now I finally figured out your recipe

It consist of wonderful looks, charm, and personality

I want to stop this fairy tale and make it a reality

And put you on love's payroll earning my heart as a salary

Your bonus will be you walking through my heart's poetry gallery

The benefits are heart conditioning, romance, and TLC

The vision to never see heartbreaks, pain, and agony

To keep focus with no interruptions or distractions

I do this from the heart to maintain my passion

The longer I look at you; I swear you got my eyes flashing

I'm just wondering what's going to be your reaction

The Day After 2morrow (New Orleans 2005)

The water's rising

All you see is people dying

Children screaming and crying

Holding on to the rooftop like it's a luxury diamond

Old people drowning

The hurricane horns are sounding

Where is the help? While the waves keep on pounding

On houses and apartment buildings

Injuring and killing our U.S. siblings

The media really don't care but they made a killing

Off this story of the year and they still not dealing

I don't see no nailing, hammering, or drilling

They were trying to survive but the media called it looting and stealing

I feel your pain and many hearts need healing

Because they called them refugees, thieves, and villains

Many of them hope not to see tents but to have walls and ceilings

Clean water, food, clothes, and a quick lottery million

They just try to blend in with everybody else like a chameleon

Without FEMA trailers and outrageous month to month crazy
billing

We as a nation shouldn't be at home relaxing and chilling

Because tomorrow we can be living outside with constant water
spilling

Hurricane Katrina
August 28, 2005

The Illustration

You're the illustration of the fountain of youth

You make my problems disappear like poof!

You're the definition of love in the physical proof

I'm in the studio of love and your heart is the booth

The paper is my microphone where I can tell you nothing but the truth

The pen is my voice and no mouth can talk with one tooth

But I can with every line I write

Every little word I recite

Because loving you can only seem right

I swear I will put up a fight

To defend the love I met that night

I will walk through Baghdad unarmed that's right

But have the hands to bring back my love despite

Of the terrorist and evils upon that militia site

No grenade will stop me from getting to my flight

Which you're the only person who can explode on me like dynamite

You're the glow of my guiding light

You make a blind man gain back all of his eyesight

Just to see the beauty of you I will use all my might

Just to hold you I will do anything to make that connection right

It's good loving that will be waiting on you tonight

The Invitation

Don't be afraid to accept my invitation

I know about the heartbreaks that led to fatal devastations

I want you to know that I got the answer to this problem, this equation

This my attack against hate my very own invasion

Don't cry because you think its betrayal but it's love is what your tasting

I know many years of disappointments, lies, drama is what you faced and

This is our opportunity to call love and demand

A piece of it even if it's just one strand

This is my request and follow, love's command

We should never fall apart because together we stand

As one and we created the first official love brand

I can't go back in the past and change the heartache land

But I do promise I'll do whatever I can

You will witness blood, sweat, and tears from this man

I hope that love will tap you shoulder and grab you by the hand

You will see love cover our beach like sand

Together forever is my future plan

The Reason Beyond Love

Love conquers all evil

Love is what we need to survive as people

Love is what makes all marriages equal

Love makes a bad relationship a happy sequel

Love is stopping me from retaliating

Love isn't spreading rumors about me so why are you hating?

Love is God so why you acting like Satan?

Love isn't war, fighting, or debating

Love is unity, trust, and communicating

Love isn't lust, porn, or masturbating

Love is something lovers keep creating

Love isn't something you should be saturating

Love is patient and always in the making

Love can leave you in suspense and have your heart shaking

Love is protection from your heart breaking

Love has its own identity there will be no mistaking

Love is always in your face but you're always steady chasing

Love away with constant dating and replacing

Love is a question that many people will be facing

Love is the answer for many relationships that are aging

Love is the reason that many hearts are inflating

Love is the right reason why we are celebrating

The Sickness

Something that you could of had

Now you can't get it and you just feeling so sad

So gone

So wrong

So depressed and all alone

No more hugs, kisses, and talking late nights on the telephone

No more candy, roses, movies, and dinner

Now you look like the loser and he's the winner

He did love you but that was ended

When you played him, he swallowed it he didn't get offended

He took his heart and just twisted it a little then bended it

Into something more caring and loving

When you see him with another woman there is nothing but mean mugging

People wonder why is she tripping? Why is she bugging?

Because now that was that woman's husband

They got a kid together and a family made

She's getting sicker because he's living it up and getting paid

Plenty of sunlight for him but she's still in the shade

Her feelings are twisted up like a braid

Now she's feeling bad because no man can compare

To him she's crying daily saying love is not fair

But I want every reader and listener to be my witness

That she's dying slowly by loves sickness

The Stalker 2

I was watching you when you took your first breath

You couldn't see me because I was hid like stealth

I watched you grow

I saw you when you wrote your first poem and your first flow

I was there when those bullets missed

I was there when you got married and gave you wife her ceremony kiss

I saw your friends and family past

But you still wonder how long your life will last

I visit so many people in Iraq and Iran

I'm just doing my job and living was never in the plan

You could be any age or any race

It's just me visiting ghettos constantly, oh man what a horrible place

They call me the Grand Reaper

A man dress with monks clothing known as life's street sweeper

I'm behind the explosions cause by Ether

Or that spread around by your English teacher

I'm living on my pulpit and I'm the preacher

Collecting souls as my tithe and offering

And giving back bodies in small and big body coffins

A… where are you going? (Death asking)

You can run now but when there is nowhere else left

Now you know you can't run and hide from me-DEATH!

The Truth

At first, it was white and black

Now it's green, red, blue, black, and the color of crack

Bandanas worn by the new hate of all colors

It was a racial thing that haunted our grandfathers and
grandmothers

Now it's the color of our clothing that have killed a lot my brothers

Cousins and many others

Dress in black leather and always equip with guns

Dress in white sheets covered in hate looking like evil nuns

They hate my skin

Like it's a sin

They hate me now and they hated us back then

Since Malcolm, Martin, Fredrick, and Harriet Tubman

Where's the minds, hearts and the meaning of tender loving

Now we're fighting over street blocks steady thuggin'

You own no blocks, your renting stop the pushing, and shoving

Dying over street numbers and street names

While the county will get all the fortune and the fame

And it's the system that you always want to blame

For not paying child support, rolling in fancy Mercedes and Bentleys

Living in the projects spending all your kids money on weed, clothes, and twenties

Not aware of life because it isn't funny

But for some reason everybody must love green the color of money

Think about it!

The World's Most Wanted

This is a story

About a woman's glory

About a woman's pain

It left a few spots even a little stain

A smart woman with so much to gain

Flying over relationships like an airplane

It's not her fault but she takes the blame

Sick of how men left and came

One out the door and things are still the same

She's all screwed up with a lot of shame

With no hope she just stuck in the same game

She wants to go right but she's stuck in the same lane

Made a wrong turn its time for a new change

Trying to shoot out love but she was out of range

With four clips of forgiveness and a target with no name

That's what happens when you're dealing love it's so strange

Thief In The Night

Get out that garbage can!

Now you wonder why you can't find a good man

The key is to stop searching

And to let your personality and image do all the working

You wondering why you always crying and hurting

Because you do too much talking and flirting

Mean mugging and smirking

Always got an attitude and being rude is what you were serving

Every good man but the bad one wasn't even deserving

You, but you kept him on your shoulder burping

Babying and spoiling but you found out he closed the curtain

That just left you out there unsure and uncertain

Why he comes only at night?

And he never comes early and bright

Never go to the movies or see the starlight's

He only needs you for sex and to start fights

He got you in check like a pair of Air Nikes

And got your head in the air like he's flying a kite

Now you see why your heart exploded like dynamite

And stole your heart like a thief in the night

This Day and Everyday

Why do I feel this way?

This day and everyday

Every month like January, February, March, April, and May

I guess this is the price I have to pay

So I get down on my knees and pray

That God bring you back to my heart today

The best place where you can relax and stay

I love it when you mold my heart like clay

You give me a hot feeling like the city of Tampa Bay

Long as I'll be with you, I know that I will be okay

This is my heart speaking and it has a lot to say

As these words of love, cruise around your mind like the Santa Fe

Or on flight to your heart and there will be no delay

Your love is home cooked from the heart and served on a tray

Unconditional Love

I'm all over your body like your Clothing

It's not just your body; it's your heart that I'm holding

It's your mind that I'm molding

You're the main reason why I have chosen

Your love before you get stolen

You got my mind spinning like tires you got me rolling

You got my blood flowing

It's nothing but love that I just keep on showing

The feeling is like a cold winter day when it's snowing

The impact is like a tornado blowing

No matter what we go through, I promise to keep going

This love is unbreakable, unconditional, and it can never be broken

I treat you like you were a shrine or a golden token

Please don't be afraid to reach out to me my hands are always open

I really want to be next to you

So close to your body like tattoo

You stand out always like a statue

Of liberty and beauty like real women do

If you don't know how much you mean to me, you should have a clue

That you're the best thing I got and I love you too

Wrong Reasons...

Do you wonder why they're cheating?

Is it because you're together for the wrong reason?

Do you wonder why he's running around here like a heathen?

And you wonder why she's talking to somebody late nights when
you're sleeping

They say it's the kids that keep them together

Or is it to avoid the county child support letter

Or they're waiting for something good knowing things will never
get better

And he was mad when he smelled some cologne on her sweater

And she was mad when he comes in the house real late

And he was mad when he came home on time to an empty house
and an empty plate

I'm just trying to advised you people out there not to make this
same mistake

It's now fast food and no more pork chops and steaks

It's a lot of cussing, fighting, broken furniture and dinner plates

No more agreeing it's just now augment debates

The household all out of shape

It feels like you been through tornado's and earthquakes

Broken car windows and house windows

Giving all your friends and family too much info.

Most of them are living the same way

But you're the new talk of the day

Next week, this month, and everyday

It was just y'all two but now everybody else wants to play

With that old saying, 'he say, she say'

Gone head home with that blasé, blasé,

Because they need to solve that drama

Before somebody will be needing medical attention or some body armor...

The Writer's Block

We been through the journey and into this boxing ring

We been talking about love, hate, life and Martin Luther King

I'm glad you had a chance to hear my heart sing

The Joy and sorrows that life will bring

This is my life, my first, my last and my everything

This isn't a one-night stand or a prostitute fling

This that Answer, that choice and the real American Dream

I'm glad you're my fans and part of my team

You helped my hopes and boosted my self-esteem

It's not all about fame or that money green

It's about change, motivation, happiness, success if you know what
I mean

To become role models, mentors, idols, and father figures

I've became a teacher, preacher, leader, and I'm not a drug dealer

I took my negativity and created this "POETIC" Creature

Just wait a while and you will see what my third book will
feature...

Coming Soon from Dreamer Publishing
Mrs. Rosette 9/27/14

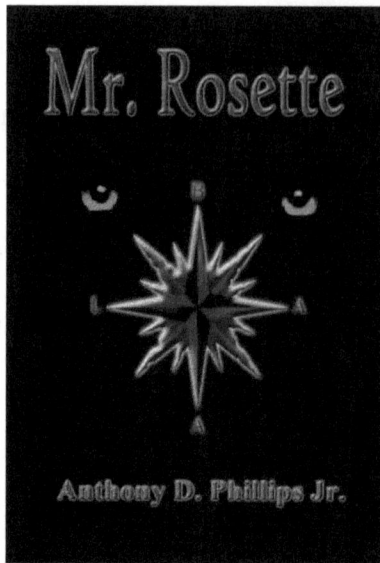

The Journey: 10 Year Deluxe Edition 12/13/14

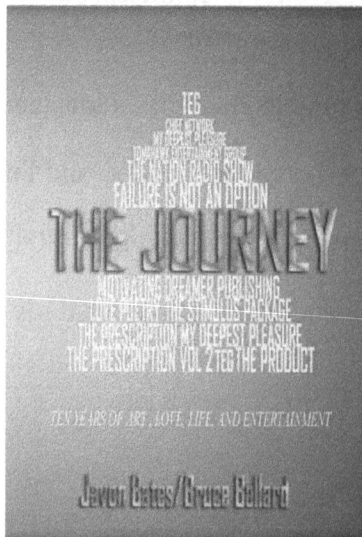

ALSO AVAILABLE FROM DREAMER PUBLISHING

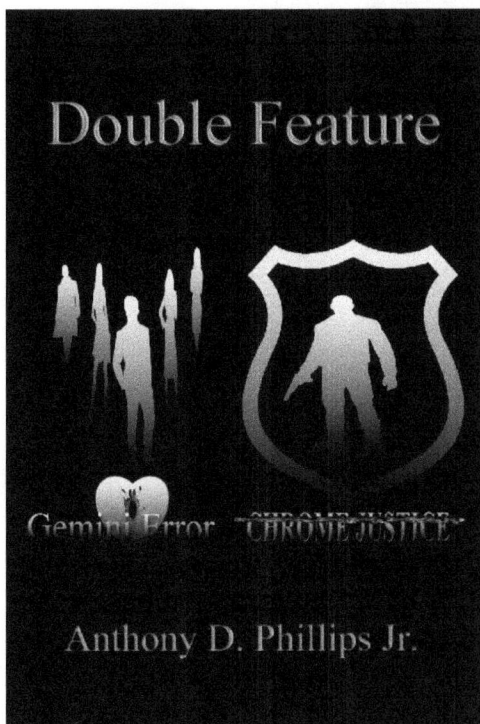

"A Double Dose of Drama"

Dreamer Publishing/Tomahawk Entertainment Group presents the new fiction double feature book entitled "Gemini Error/Chrome Justice" by author Anthony D. Phillips Jr. The reader favorite Gemini Error, returns in a new edition featuring Chrome Justice, an action packed crime drama that will keep readers on the edge of their seats and wanting more!

Gemini Error

Harold Atkins is on top of the world. On the surface, his life seems perfect, but underneath that perfection, there is a dirty secret, another life! A tangled web of sex and lies will take him to a point of no return and destroy everything that he has worked so hard to build.

Chrome Justice

Sometimes... justice can only be achieved through violence. Robert Cross is living the good life at the expense of others. Herrick Hunter is determined to put a stop to it. While most of the city's population live in fear and look the other way, Herrick refuses to do so. He has a score to settle, deaths to avenge and justice to deliver. www.adpbooks.com